Sara

# Shrews

*Ant*

© 1986 The Mammal Society
First published in 1986 by Anthony Nelson Ltd
PO Box 9, Oswestry, Shropshire SY11 1BY, England.

Series editor Robert Burton
Diagrams by Jean Vaughan: 7, 12, 13, 15, 17 (13 by permission of the
Zoological Society of London)
Drawings by Robert Gillmor (from *The Handbook of British Mammals*,
Blackwells, 1977): 4, 5; Graham Allen: 12, 19
Photographs by Jane Burton: front cover, 10; David Hosking: inside
back cover (top); Pat Morris: inside front cover, 1, 3, inside back
cover (bottom), back cover

Royalties from this series will go to the Mammal Society

ISBN 0 904614 15 8

Designed by Alan Bartram
Printed by Livesey Ltd, 7 St John's Hill, Shrewsbury

Cover *Common shrew*
Inside front cover
*Top: lesser white-tailed shrew*
*Bottom: pygmy shrew*

Shrews are easily recognised by their long, pointed noses, tiny eyes and dense velvety fur, which show them to be different from mice and voles. They belong to the family Soricidae, and are insectivores related to the mole and hedgehog. There are over 200 species distributed throughout most of the world from North America, through Europe, Africa, Asia to Japan. Some are almost as large as rats but the majority are mouse-sized and the Etruscan shrew is one of the smallest of all known mammals, adults weighing only 2 grams.

Shrews have been the subject of many ancient superstitions. For example, a shrew walking over sleeping cattle was thought to cause lameness, and horses or cattle feeding in pastures occupied by shrews were sure to die. In fact, the name *araneus* (Latin for spider) was given to shrews because they were thought to be poisonous like a spider. The Romans were convinced that shrews were evil and even in the seventeenth century, the natural historian Topsell described the shrew as 'a ravening beast, feigning itself gentle and tame, but being touched it biteth deep, and poisoneth deadly. It beareth a cruel mind'. Antidotes were developed to protect people and their animals from the shrew's evil effects. To keep cattle or horses safe from a shrew's bite it was necessary to pack a shrew's body in lime until dry and hard and hang it around the neck of the beast.

So, from early times shrews had a bad reputation, not only for their apparently evil influence but also for their bad temper and ferocity which lead to the notorious shrewish character as portrayed in literature.

In contrast, shrews also gained a reputation for being feeble, highly-strung

*Species of shrew compared: (a) common shrew; (b) pygmy shrew; (c) water shrew; (d) lesser white-toothed shrew.*

and subject to shock. It was said that a shrew would drop dead at the sight of a human being and that a shrew could not cross the path of a human and live. They were thought to die of fright if handled or subjected to loud noises. We know considerably more about the habits of shrews than did the early naturalists, so what is the truth about these enigmatic beasts?

## Appearance and distribution

In Britain there are five species of shrew of which the common shrew *Sorex araneus* is the most familiar. The adults are dark brown with pale bellies and they occasionally have tufts of white fur on the ears. They have a body length of 48–71 millimetres and a tail length of 24–44 millimetres. Adults may weigh up to 13.0 grams, but juveniles are considerably smaller at 5–7 grams and they are usually a lighter brown before their first moult. Common shrews are found throughout mainland Britain and many of the islands, with the exception of the Outer Hebrides, Shetland and Ireland.

The smallest of the British shrews is the pygmy shrew *Sorex minutus* which weighs only 2.3–5.0 grams and is about as heavy as a 1p piece. It has a body length of 40–55 millimetres and is brown in colour. It may be distinguished from the common shrew not only by its much smaller size but also by its relatively longer and more hairy tail. It, too, is found throughout mainland Britain and most of the islands but it is absent from Shetland, the Scillies and

*The anterior teeth of shrews: (a) common shrew; (b) pygmy shrew; (c) water shrew; (d) greater white-toothed shrew. Note the red tips on the teeth of the first three species.*

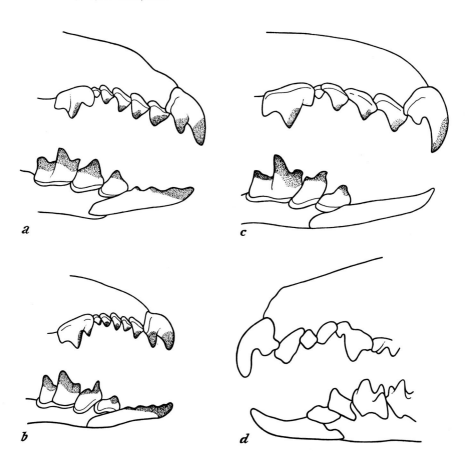

the Channel Islands. Interestingly enough, it is the only species of shrew to be found in Ireland.

The most elusive of our native shrews is the water shrew *Neomys fodiens*. It is also the largest, weighing 9.0–16.0 grams. It usually has a black back, white belly and white tufts of fur around the eyes and ears which makes this species the most handsome of shrews. It receives its name from its amphibious habits. Associated with these are the fringes of stiff hairs along the edge of the hind feet and the underside of the tail which are thought to assist in swimming and diving under water. Water shrews occur throughout the British mainland and most of the islands but they tend to have a localised and sporadic distribution.

The lesser and greater white-toothed shrews, as their name implies, lack the red enamel on the crowns of the teeth that is so characteristic of the other British shrews. The lesser white-toothed shrew *Crocidura suaveolens* is about the size of a common shrew but its fur is reddish-brown in colour and it possesses larger ears. In Britain, it is only found on the Scilly Isles and on Jersey and Sark of the Channel Islands. Its close relative, the greater white-toothed shrew *Crocidura russula* is slightly larger but otherwise very similar in outward appearance. It inhabits the Channel Islands of Alderney, Guernsey and Herm.

## Signs

Shrews are not easy to observe in the wild because of their small size and the dense cover in which they live. However, they may occasionally be seen bustling through the undergrowth along a hedgerow, particularly in summer. Shrews inhabit burrows and those of water shrews are the easiest to locate because they have characteristically small, rounded entrances in the banks of streams.

Shrews are more frequently heard than seen, and can be detected by the high-pitched shrieks and chatters given when they meet each other, particularly in summer when they are very active on the ground surface and searching for mates. Even so, their calls may be so high-pitched that they are beyond the hearing range of most older people.

Water shrews have the habit of leaving remains of prey, such as mollusc shells or the cases of caddis larvae, at a favourite feeding spot on a stone or on the bank of a stream. They also leave piles of black droppings at intervals along their runways through the vegetation.

## Where shrews live

Shrews are typically terrestrial and are widely distributed in Britain where they are found almost anywhere, living among ground vegetation and leaf litter in woodlands, grasslands, scrub and hedgerows. They even inhabit hedge bottoms, compost heaps and other rough places in gardens, and may be attracted by morsels of food dropped from bird tables. They generally prefer places with plenty of ground cover, where they can find food and avoid predators.

Common and pygmy shrews mostly inhabit deciduous woodland, hedgerows and scrub-grassland. Water shrews also occur in such places, often several kilometres from water, but they are most frequently found on the grassy banks of rivers, streams, ponds and drainage ditches. Watercress beds are a favourite habitat for these shrews.

White-toothed shrews are found wherever there is sufficient cover and food, particularly in grassy habitats on sand dunes. On the Scilly Isles, they are common among rocks on the seashore. White-toothed shrews may also occur around dwellings, hence they are sometimes called house-shrews.

*Proportions of major prey types in the diets of shrews.*

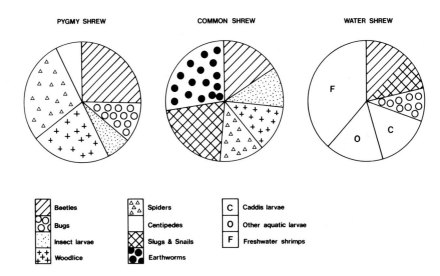

PYGMY SHREW COMMON SHREW WATER SHREW

| | | |
|---|---|---|
| Beetles | Spiders | C Caddis larvae |
| Bugs | Centipedes | O Other aquatic larvae |
| Insect larvae | Slugs & Snails | F Freshwater shrimps |
| Woodlice | Earthworms | |

Shrews inhabit underground burrow systems but venture out on to the ground surface to forage and find mates. They are not good burrowers themselves and they often use and modify the tunnels of other small mammals. They may make their nest in a tunnel or in grass tussocks beneath fallen logs and similar places.

## Feeding habits

Shrews are predominantly insectivorous but they take a wide variety of prey ranging from tiny springtails, no more than 3 millimetres long, to large earthworms of over 60 millimetres. Common shrews feed on most terrestrial invertebrates including earthworms, slugs, snails, centipedes, bugs and flies but the most important items in the diet are usually adult beetles, insect larvae and woodlice. Occasionally, small quantities of plant material may be eaten.

Pygmy shrews have similar feeding habits but they tend to catch slightly smaller prey on average than common shrews. Their main prey are beetles, spiders, woodlice, flies and bugs. A notable difference between the feeding habits of these two shrews is that pygmy shrews never eat earthworms in the wild, possibly because they are generally too large to tackle.

Water shrews also eat a wide variety of terrestrial invertebrates such as beetles, spiders, molluscs and earthworms, and thus overlap considerably with common and pygmy shrews. If they are living far away from water they will subsist entirely on terrestrial prey, but when close to water they augment the diet with aquatic invertebrates, particularly freshwater shrimps, water slaters, caddis larvae and fly larvae. They are even known to take small fish, newts and frogs. They forage underwater throughout the year, regardless of the weather, but never feed entirely on aquatic prey: usually these prey comprise about 50 per cent of the diet and never more than about 67 per cent.

The feeding habits of white-toothed shrews are very similar to those of common shrews with a wide variety of invertebrates being eaten. In addition, lesser white-toothed shrews eat large numbers of amphipod crustaceans living amongst rocks on the seashore. Despite their small size, greater white-toothed shrews have been known to catch and eat lizards and small rodents.

Despite their catholic feeding habits, shrews do discriminate between different prey and show preference for some and distaste for others. For example, millipedes are not favoured as food because of their acrid secretion, and some molluscs, including the garden slug *Arion hortensis*, are not much liked because of their slime. Such molluscs are eaten only when the slime has been rubbed off with the shrew's forefeet or wiped off against the ground. Bristly caterpillars and strongly armoured prey, such as beetles and snails, may be left if other prey are available. Some woodlice are preferred to others; for common shrews, *Philoscia* is the most palatable while *Armadillidium*, with its thick exoskeleton, is least preferred.


## How much do they eat?

Shrews are renowned for their voracious appetites. They have to eat frequently, every two to three hours throughout day and night, to survive. They also need large quantities of food, although different species require different amounts of food, generally according to their body weight. For example a water shrew eats approximately half its body weight in food every 24 hours, a common shrew requires about 70 per cent of its body weight and the tiny pygmy shrew consumes 1¼ times its own weight each day. The exceptions are the white-toothed shrews which eat considerably less than might be expected on the basis of body weight alone (only about half their body weight). This is probably due to their slightly lower metabolic rate.

However, these estimates of food consumption do not take into account the large proportion of water present in prey: most invertebrates comprise at least 70 per cent water. If the food consumption of a shrew living on maggots is compared with a mouse of similar size feeding on dry seeds, they both eat approximately the same amount in terms of the dry weight of food eaten per day. Moreover, most invertebrates have a large amount of indigestible, chitinous exoskeleton.

Consequently, a common shrew has to find and eat around 100 maggot-sized prey every 24 hours. How do shrews manage to find sufficient prey? Their catholic and opportunist feeding habits means that they can eat almost anything available and, in fact, invertebrates are extremely numerous. There are up to a thousand potential prey animals per square metre among the vegetation and the underlying soil in scrub-grassland, a typical shrew habitat. Even in winter there is no shortage of food, although finding it may be difficult in frosty conditions.

## Foraging behaviour

Shrews spend most of their time foraging, and are very efficient hunters. Their ability to find prey quickly is quite remarkable: captive common shrews, for example, can locate and dig out inactive dormant prey such as insect pupae buried up to 12 centimetres deep in soil. I watched a shrew as it foraged among short grass and moss and within 15 minutes it had found and eaten one earthworm, a cranefly larva, a large caterpillar and a slug, in an area of about 3 square metres. All these animals had been hidden from view. Shrews' tiny eyes are probably of little use for finding prey but their sense of smell is much better developed and they have sensitive snouts furnished with touch-sensitive whiskers. It seems that a combination of smell, touch and hearing, and very thorough but random searching are used to locate prey. The shrews run over the ground, furrowing through the leaf litter and undergrowth, stopping at intervals to probe with their snouts and dig with their forefeet. Even flying insects can be captured: I once saw a pygmy shrew jump into the air repeatedly after a bluebottle fly, until it was knocked to the ground and pounced on.

When an animal has been caught, the shrew bites its head to immobilise it and then eats it, usually from the head down. Certain parts may not be eaten, and large wings, legs and other unpalatable parts are usually discarded. Captive shrews sometimes cache surplus food in the nest or in a small depression in the ground which they cover with leaves. They probably do this in the wild when there is a superabundance of prey, but the difficulties of observing shrews in natural conditions means that the habit has never been recorded in the wild.

Occasionally a shrew will curl up on its side or back, usually when in the nest during day-time rest periods. With hind limbs apart, it proceeds to lick its anus, then everts the rectum and spends several minutes licking it. This habit, called refection, has been likened to the habit of coprophagy, or eating the droppings, in rabbits and rats, but shrews only lick up a milky, white fluid from the rectum. However, refection probably has the similar function of extracting more nutrients from food by passing it through the gut twice.

All shrews can swim but only water shrews hunt underwater. They do this by swimming along the surface then diving to the bottom, searching among the stones and submerged plants with snout and forefeet, picking up an animal in the mouth, and carrying it out to the bank or a nearby rock before killing and eating it. Although water shrews can dive to over 1 metre in

depth, the length of each dive is extremely short, in the order of 4 seconds. They are very buoyánt because of their rounded shape and the layer of air trapped by the fur. Hence they have to paddle hard to stay underwater for long, and they may hold on to rocks or plants in order to stay submerged. Hunting is most efficient in shallow water where less time has to be spent diving and returning to the surface. Shallow water, coupled with the abundance of suitable prey and the clean conditions, may be the reason why watercress beds are so popular with water shrews.

Many dives end with no prey being caught, and some end with the wrong objects being retrieved. It is common for both wild and captive water shrews to confuse pieces of twig, plant stems, small stones and empty caddis larvae cases for live prey. The mistake is only realised when the shrew returns to land with the object. So, in conclusion, foraging underwater is probably very energy-consuming and inefficient but it may be a good way to avoid competition with other species of shrew. There is evidence that water shrews produce a toxic secretion in the saliva, which probably helps to immobilise the prey, particularly amphibians, fish and larger invertebrates. The venom mainly effects the nervous system and, when injected into mice, causes convulsions, paralysis of limbs, and respiratory and blood pressure disorders.

## Breeding

Shrews are essentially solitary animals and only during the breeding season in spring and summer do they make close contact with each other. Shrews generally mature in the spring (March and April) following their birth in the previous summer and are then ready to mate. The males search for females but attempts to mate are frequently met with fierce rebuffs accompanied by a great deal of loud squeaking and scuffling. Only during the brief period of oestrus, which may last for a mere 24 hours, is the female receptive to the advances of the male and willing to mate with him. Mating is brief, during which time the male mounts the female and uses his teeth to hold her by the scruff of the neck or the top of the head. As a result, mated females can usually be distinguished by a small, bare patch here. After mating, the male shows no further interest in his mate but wanders off and contributes nothing to the upbringing of the young.

Despite their reputation for ferocity, female shrews are careful and diligent mothers. The young are born between May and September after a gestation period of approximately three weeks. The female constructs a large, domed nest of leaves and dried grass beneath a log, in a grass tussock or in an underground burrow. Here she bears three to nine young which are born blind and hairless, each weighing about 0.5 grams. They grow very rapidly and within a week or so are able to crawl around the nest. If they fall or climb out of the nest, their squeaks of distress will alert the mother and she will hurry out to find them. They are carried back to the nest in her mouth when they are very small, or dragged by the scruff of the neck as they become larger.

After nine days, the fur of young common shrews becomes evident as a grey down and by 11 days the teeth show their characteristic red tips. By 14 days of age the young each weigh 5–7 grams, are covered in short, fine, greyish fur and their eyes are beginning to open. This is a very busy time for the mother who must feed herself as well as her young. When she is not nursing the young she is out foraging and her food intake increases dramatically to about 120 per cent of her body weight per day.

By 16 days of age the eyes of the young are fully open and thereafter they begin to venture out of the nest for short periods. At approximately 21 days old they begin to catch and eat invertebrate prey, but they still attempt to get milk from their mother. She can be heard making threatening calls when they are too persistent. At 22–25 days old the young shrews are fully weaned and nearly full grown, and they are encouraged to leave the nest by the mother, who becomes increasingly hostile towards them. The young also show aggression towards each other and within a few days of weaning they disperse to find their own nesting sites and become fully independent.

For a limited period when the litter is well-grown, the young shrews may follow their mother in a 'caravan'. This habit is characteristic of white-toothed shrews, but has also been observed in common shrews, and it is

*Top: The growth of young common shrews. They lose weight at weaning while they learn to find their own food.*
*Bottom: A litter of shrews 'caravanning' behind their mother.*

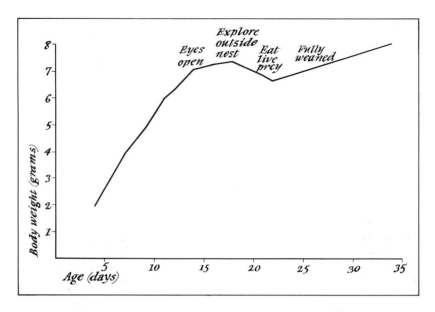

often associated with disturbance of the nest. Stimulated by the mother, each one grasps the base of the tail of the preceding shrew so that the mother runs along with a line of young trailing behind. In this way they are conveyed safely and quickly to a new nest. It may also be used to encourage exploration and extend the young shrews' knowledge of the environment once they are large enough to move about.

The female shrew will probably mate again after the litter has dispersed and may produce two or possibly three litters during the course of a summer.

The young go through a number of stages when they are particularly vulnerable. The female is unlikely to be able to rear all the young in a large litter. Captive shrews, for example, generally manage to rear only three or four young. The first week or so after birth is a critical time for a young shrew in a large litter. Growth is rapid but it varies between litter-mates and the smallest and weakest succumb in the competition for food. It seems that weaning is a difficult time because young shrews lose weight after they have been rejected by the mother, probably because they have to learn to find their own food. These inexperienced shrews are also particularly vulnerable to predation.

12

*Survival curves of young shrews based on studies of marked individuals: about 50 per cent apparently die within the first two months.*

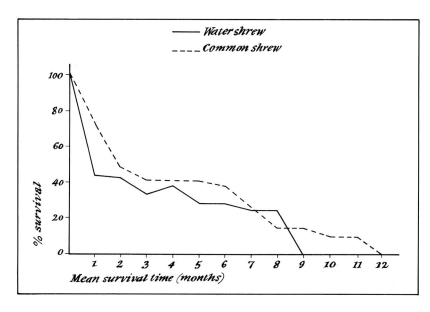

## Lifespan

Shrews are very short-lived compared with many animals of similar size such as mice. The adults die after breeding and the young carry the population through the winter and into the following year, when it will be their turn to breed. In the wild, common shrews are extremely lucky to reach the extreme old age of 12 months, and pygmy shrews have a similar lifespan. Although a few water shrews may live up to 19 months in the wild, they may have a higher average mortality rate than common shrews. White-toothed shrews have a slightly longer lifespan than the other species, for example greater white-toothed shrews have been known to survive for 1½ years in the wild. All shrews can live longer in captivity, the record being four years for a greater white-toothed shrew.

## Seasonal population cycles and survival

Shrews undergo seasonal cycles in population numbers, and these are particularly marked in common and pygmy shrews. The shrew population reaches a peak in summer when breeding occurs and there are many juveniles about. It declines rapidly in autumn and remains at a low level through the winter before breeding commences in the following spring. The magnitude of these seasonal cycles differs from year to year and may also vary according to the habitat.

The rapid decline in shrew numbers in autumn has been of great interest to naturalists for many years. It is so dramatic that it was once thought to be

13

due to some mysterious disease or parasite and it became known as the 'autumnal epidemic'. When live-trapping techniques permitted a much closer and more detailed look at the fate of individually-marked shrews, studies showed that the rapid mortality occurs in autumn (October to November), mostly before the onset of winter weather conditions, and that there are two main causes. By this time the old adults have finished breeding and they die, simply from the effects of old age, such as worn teeth and an inability to compete with younger, fitter animals. There is also very high mortality of inexperienced juveniles which is coupled with their dispersal away from the study area. Approximately 50 per cent of common shrews disappear in this way within the first two months of life. Many are taken by predators as they establish new home-ranges and search for suitable nest sites. So the cause of the 'autumnal epidemic' has quite a simple explanation.

What happens to shrews in winter-time? Shrews are not seen or heard very often at this time of year, and many people suppose that they either die or hibernate. In fact, about 20–30 per cent of the juveniles survive to breed the following spring and, once winter is reached, shrews survive surprisingly well and their mortality rate is actually lower in this season than at any other time of year.

Shrews do not hibernate because they are too small and are unable to store sufficient fat to keep them going during long periods of inactivity. However, it does seem that they become much less active above ground in cold weather and they move around less. Marked shrews have disappeared for months on end and suddenly re-emerged at their original capture sites as spring comes on, but where they have been is a mystery.

## Population size

Population densities vary considerably according to the species of shrew, the nature of the habitat and the season. Common shrews, as their name implies, are the most numerous shrews in Britain. Maximum numbers occur in summer, typically from about 20 per hectare in scrubland to 70 per hectare in grassland and deciduous woodland. Winter population densities in these habitats are smaller, between 5 and 30 per hectare respectively.

Pygmy shrews are less numerous: in the order of 8 per hectare in woodland and up to 40 per hectare in grassland during the summer, but down to 4 per hectare or less in winter. Even in Ireland, where no other shrew species are present, they have lower population densities than common shrews.

The population densities of water shrews are extremely difficult to estimate because these shrews tend to move about a lot and they often live in small groups. They are by no means common and, even in favoured sites like watercress beds, they only achieve densities of about 3 per hectare.

*Seasonal changes in the population density of shrews: the numbers of common and pygmy shrews captured in successive months in 1.5 hectares of scrub-grassland.*

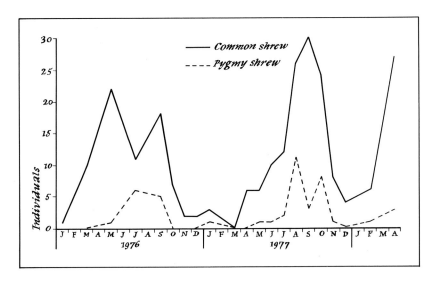

Neither of the white-toothed shrews are very numerous in the British Isles, and their population densities are rather lower than those of pygmy shrews.

## Home-ranges and territories

Shrews maintain home-ranges to which they confine their activities. Here they nest, forage and explore. Whether such areas can be called territories in the strict sense of the word is debatable. There is insufficient evidence to show that wild shrews actively defend an area against intruders and the home-ranges of different individuals frequently overlap, at least in part, especially during the breeding season when males are travelling around in search of females. On the other hand, there is some evidence to suggest that their home-ranges may be mutually exclusive, particularly in winter, and captive common shrews will certainly chase others away from their own home areas.

Male and female common shrews maintain home-ranges of similar sizes. These home-ranges are smaller in winter than in summer but generally they occupy areas of up to 900 square metres. When young shrews become independent from their parents they move around for a while before adopting a particular area as the home-range. This area is maintained in much the same location throughout the life of most shrews. In fact, common shrews may be captured in the same small area month after month from youth through to old age. However, nomadic behaviour becomes more apparent in the breeding season, particularly in males who may travel over 100 metres from their normal home-range area in the search for mates.

Pygmy shrews have similar habits but, despite their smaller size, they have larger home-ranges than common shrews, in the order of 500–1800 square metres. These large home-ranges are maintained even in the absence of other shrew species which may compete for space and resources, as for example in Ireland.

The home-range size of water shrews has not been easy to ascertain because they are difficult to catch and they have nomadic tendencies. They frequently live in small groups and so their home-ranges often overlap. White-toothed shrews also have overlapping home-ranges. Males of the lesser white-toothed shrew have home-ranges of 50 metres or less in diameter while those of females are only about 27 metres in diameter.

## Activity rhythms

Shrews must feed regularly every few hours or they will die. Hence, they must be active both by day and by night but, even so, they are not active all the time. They have bouts of activity, lasting from 30 minutes to some 2 hours, during which they forage and explore, alternating with periods of rest of similar length spent in the nest. Sometimes, a period of intense activity may be interrupted by a sudden desire for a rest. Rather than return to the nest, a shrew may have a quick cat-nap wherever it happens to be. During this time it remains motionless with head and nose tucked up against the chest. After a few seconds it will wake up and resume its activities.

Longer periods of rest are spent in the nest, but even here a shrew will not remain totally inactive for long. Complete rest lasts only minutes at a time and is interrupted by periods of grooming, modifying the nest or having a quick snack of food from a cache.

Common and water shrews are most active during the night and at dawn and dusk, and they are least active around midday and early afternoon. Pygmy shrews have a similar pattern of activity, but each alternating active and resting periods tends to be shorter than in common shrews. Pygmy shrews are equally active by day and by night, being more active during daytime than common shrews.

The activity of shrews is to some extent affected by the weather. Although wild shrews must venture out to forage at frequent intervals, they are less active when it is wet and cold. This is particularly evident as winter approaches and they become much less active on the surface of the ground. Captive shrews exposed to cold, wet conditions tend to spend much longer in the nest and come out only for short bouts of activity.

*Changes in body weight of common shrews through their lifetime. Note the sudden decrease in weight as winter approaches.*

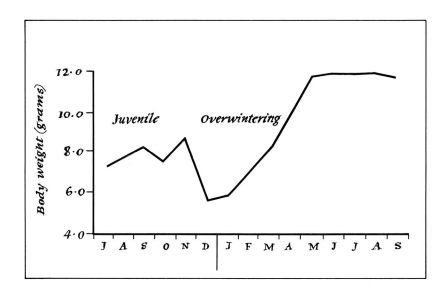

## Seasonal weight changes

Shrews, especially common, pygmy and water shrews, undergo seasonal changes in body weight with a marked decrease during winter. For example, young common shrews born during the summer achieve weights of 7–8 grams by September-October. They overwinter as immature animals and, as winter approaches, they suddenly decrease in weight to as little as 5½ grams. Frequently, this weight loss is in the order of 27 per cent which is equivalent to a reduction from 50 kilograms to 31 kilograms in a human. Body weight reaches a minimum between December and February and then shrews rapidly gain weight in March–April as they grow and become sexually mature, and by summer they weigh 10–12 grams.

How are these weight changes manifested? The decrease in weight is brought about in part by changes in dimensions of the skeleton, notably the cranium, and of certain internal organs such as the adrenal bodies, as well as a reduction in body water content. However, these changes do not fully account for the shrew's loss in weight in winter and it still remains something of a mystery.

The cause of this phenomenon has been the subject of much speculation. For many years it was assumed that the weight loss was the result of reduced food supply in cold, winter conditions. However, recent studies have shown that the seasonal weight change of shrews cannot be attributed to this because, in fact, food supply is not depleted in winter (although it may be difficult for shrews to forage in frosty conditions). Secondly, captive shrews in outdoor enclosures with a plentiful and easily accessible food supply still

17

lose weight in winter. Temperature and daylength may provide cues for changes in body weight but the exact cause has yet to be explained. One suggestion is that the loss of weight may be a way of reducing food requirements in winter: a small shrew eats less prey than a large shrew and so has to devote less time to foraging in the cold. This could make a difference to a common shrew, for example, of about 20 maggot-sized prey per day. It does not sound very much, but it could be significant for a shrew that cannot hibernate but must feed daily throughout the winter.

Another strange phenomenon is the inability of wild shrews to store up fat to any extent. Captive shrews, on the other hand, often become quite obese as a result of a constant food supply, warm conditions and lack of exercise. It seems that wild shrews have such a busy and stressful life that they never get fat. Perhaps there are lessons to be learned from shrews about the causes and control of obesity in man.

## Communication and social interactions

Shrews are generally unsociable and they tend to avoid each other. Scent-marking is a means of communication used by shrews to avoid direct contact with each other. Shrews produce a strong, musky smell from a gland on each flank between the fore- and hind-legs. These glands are present in both sexes throughout the year but are most obvious in mature males. They are small, oval areas of skin rich in blood vessels and containing many sebaceous and sweat glands, and bordered by stiff hairs. They produce a greasy secretion which sticks to the overlying fur and rubs off on to the vegetation and the walls of burrows as the shrew passes by. The function may be to mark out a territory and discourage strangers. This is supported by the fact that the flank glands of females in breeding condition are poorly developed so that males are not discouraged from seeking to mate with them.

Scent is also produced from anal glands and deposited with the droppings. Hence, scent-marking may occur by strategic placing of the droppings, for example, around the borders of a territory or home-range. Captive shrews usually deposit their droppings around the edges of their cages, often in middens in the far corners.

Communication between shrews also occurs by means of calls. These take two main forms. One is the soft but high-pitched twitters frequently emitted as a shrew explores and forages. Similar sounds are used between the female and her young. The other form is the much louder and more raucous, staccato squeaks produced when a shrew is alarmed or angry, and these squeaks or shrieks are employed when two shrews meet. Both shrews face each other with head up, mouth open and snout contracted, and each squeaks loudly and repeatedly to warn off the other as a preliminary to physical combat. Such vocal sparring may be sufficient to discourage further contact and make one or other of the shrews retreat.

*Aggressive postures of common shrews are accompanied by squeaking, and may be followed by a fight.*

Some of the sounds produced by shrews, particularly those of *Sorex* species, are ultrasounds which have a frequency too high for human ears. There is some evidence that these ultrasounds are used in echolocation, especially when shrews are exploring new areas, and they may provide details about the environment in the form of an 'acoustic image'. However, shrews' echolocating abilities can only be crude and function over a short range. They are unlikely to assist in the location of prey in their cluttered habitats of plant roots and stems, leaf litter, stones and logs. White-toothed shrews show no signs of using echolocation.

Common and pygmy shrews are very aggressive and calling is frequently followed by rough scuffles which, if in a confined space, may prove fatal. When two shrews meet, a sequence of events unfurls. Initially they both freeze, then loud squeaking commences and they rear up on their hind legs. If a fight starts, they first aim bites at each other's heads, after which one may throw itself on its back while continuing to squeak and kick, and the other then rushes off into the undergrowth. If fighting continues, they aim bites at each other's tails while hitting out with the forelegs. Sometimes they may become locked in combat before one breaks loose and retreats.

Not all shrews are equally aggressive. White-toothed shrews, for example, are much more sociable than other species and frequently share the same nest, even if of the same sex, and small groups can be kept together quite amicably. Water shrews can also be kept together provided they are given sufficient space: they do not share nests but each will make its own nest and adopt its own small area where an intruder is not welcome. Interactions are confined to loud calls as a protest against intruding neighbours, and scuffles ensue only if the intruder gets too close.

What happens when one shrew meets another of a different species? Although different species frequently live in the same area, it seems that they ignore each other and avoid direct contact.

## Parasites

Shrews are hosts for a wide variety of parasites, both inside and out. While they may be of some annoyance and inconvenience to the shrew, they are generally harmless and, moreover, are not generally transmissable to man. The most obvious parasites are different species of fleas, such as *Palaeopsylla soricis* and *Doratopsylla dasycnema*, which are large and easily spotted in the fur. Despite a shrew's small size, it may carry several of these parasites, especially in summer when the population densities of both shrews and parasites are high. Mites are commonly found hidden amongst the dense fur but are too tiny to be seen easily with the naked eye.

Inside, shrews are a parasitologist's dream. They harbour large numbers of different digenean flukes, tapeworms and nematodes in the stomach and gut. The numbers of parasites present vary according to the age of the shrew and the season: it is not uncommon to find over 200 tapeworms in the gut of an old shrew in midsummer. Another parasite which often occurs is *Porrocaecum talpae*, a nematode worm which lies coiled up under the skin of shrews and whose final host is an owl.

The reason why shrews harbour such a high diversity and density of parasites lies in their feeding habits. Many of their prey, particularly beetles, slugs and snails, act as intermediate hosts of these internal parasites which are then transmitted to a shrew as it eats its prey.

## Predators

The major predators of shrews are tawny owls and barn owls. Stoats, weasels and foxes are known to take shrews, and kestrels may also prey upon them. They even fall prey to fish occasionally: their remains have been found in considerable numbers in the stomachs of the grayling in Russia. Domestic cats frequently catch and kill shrews but will not eat them. Shrews are unpalatable to many predators, including cats, because of the smell from their scent glands, particularly those on the flanks, but this is hardly any consolation to a shrew once it is dead. There is no evidence that cats, for example, learn not to kill shrews because they are distasteful to eat, so their musky scent is unlikely to provide much protection from predators.